AMSTERDAM TRAVEL GUIDE 2023

The Complete Pocket guide for first timers to plan where to stay, What Activities to Engage in, where to visit in Netherlands and How to Plan an Unforgettable Trip

Chad C. Wood

Copyright © 2023 Chad Wood

All rights reserved. No part of this publication may be reproduced, distributed, or transmitted in any form or by any means, including photocopying, recording, or other electronic or mechanical methods, without the prior written permission of the publisher, except in the case of brief quotations embodied in critical reviews and certain other noncommercial uses permitted by copyright law.

Table of Contents

Introduction

Origin of Amsterdam

Chapter One

Before You Go

Amsterdam's Climate and what to expect during Your Visit

Necessary Entry Requirements and Visas

Currency and Payment Options

Language and Basic Phrases

Amsterdam City's Public Transportation System and How to Get Around

Chapter Two

Where to Stay

Chapter Three

Top Attractions and Activities

The Van Gogh Museum

Rijksmuseum

Anne Frank House

A Canal Cruise

Vondelpark

Jordaan District

Red Light District

Chapter Four

Where to Eat

Dutch Traditional Dishes

Best Restaurants and Food Markets

Vegan and Vegetarian Delights

Chapter Five

Nightlife and Entertainment

Bars and Pubs:

Concerts and Music Venues:

Coffeeshops:

Chapter Six

Day Trips from Amsterdam

Zaanse Schans: A Step Back in Time

Keukenhof Gardens: A Floral Paradise

Utrecht: Canals and Charm

Haarlem: Art and Culture

Rotterdam: Modern Marvels

The Hague: Royal and Political Hub

Giethoorn: Venice of the North

Chapter Seven

Tips for an Unforgettable Trip

Appendix

Essential Contact Information

Public Holidays in the Netherlands (2023)

Introduction

If you're considering a trip to this enchanting destination in 2023, you're in for an unforgettable experience. Amsterdam, the capital of the Netherlands, is a city that seamlessly blends rich history with a modern, forward-thinking spirit. From its iconic canals, world-class museums, and diverse neighborhoods, there's something to captivate every traveler.

Amsterdam holds timeless allure, but there are plenty of exciting reasons to visit this year. 2023 marks a significant milestone for the city, celebrating its 750th anniversary. Join the festivities as Amsterdam showcases its unique cultural heritage, artistic treasures, and innovations that have shaped the city into what it is today. From special exhibitions to cultural events, the celebratory atmosphere will add an extra layer of magic to your journey.

Moreover, Amsterdam consistently ranks as one of the most bike-friendly cities globally, making it an ideal destination for eco-conscious travelers. Explore the charming streets, cycle along scenic routes, and discover hidden gems while contributing to sustainable tourism practices.

This guide has been thoughtfully curated to assist you in planning an incredible trip to Amsterdam. Whether you're a first-time visitor or returning to rediscover the city's charm, we've got you covered. Here's a breakdown of what you can expect:

Discover Must-visit attractions, including world-renowned museums like the Van Gogh Museum and the Anne Frank House, Where to Stay and Dine, Exciting Activities and Entertainment.

To make the most of your Amsterdam adventure, consider factors such as the best time to visit, essential phrases to ease communication, and cultural etiquette. Familiarize yourself with the public transportation system, and get tips on sustainable travel to support the city's efforts in preserving its beauty for generations to come.

Now, with this guide in hand, you're ready to embark on a journey through the unique charms of Amsterdam. So, let's dive in

Origin of Amsterdam

Amsterdam's origins can be traced back to the 12th century when a small fishing village emerged near the Amstel River. The city's name, "Amsterdam," is derived from a combination of "Amstel" and "dam," referencing the river's location and the dam that was constructed to protect the settlement from the river's flooding.

In the 13th century, Amsterdam started to flourish as a trading hub, thanks to its strategic location and access to waterways connecting it to other European cities. The residents-built canals to enhance trade and transportation, which laid the foundation for Amsterdam's iconic canal system that we admire today.

By the 17th century, known as the Dutch Golden Age, Amsterdam had become one of the wealthiest and most influential cities in the world. The Dutch East India Company, headquartered in Amsterdam, played a pivotal role in global trade, bringing immense prosperity to the city and its merchants.

During this period, Amsterdam also embraced cultural and intellectual developments, fostering the growth of art, literature, and sciences. Legendary painters like Rembrandt and Vermeer left their mark, leaving behind a treasure trove of masterpieces that can be admired in museums to this day.

As the city continued to grow, its tolerance and openness to different cultures attracted diverse communities, making Amsterdam a melting pot of ideas and perspectives. The city became a haven for those seeking religious freedom, with a reputation for welcoming people from various backgrounds.

Over time, Amsterdam expanded beyond its original boundaries, adding new neighborhoods and landmarks. The 19th and 20th centuries saw the construction of iconic buildings, such as the Rijksmuseum and the Concertgebouw, further solidifying Amsterdam's status as a center of art and culture.

Today, Amsterdam is a modern city that values its old traditions while also welcoming new ideas and taking care of the environment. When you explore the streets and feel the lively atmosphere, you'll be connecting with the city's history that made Amsterdam the charming place it is now.

Before You Go

Amsterdam's Climate and what to expect during Your Visit

Amsterdam's climate is characterized by mild summers, cool winters, and a fair amount of rainfall throughout the year. To fully enjoy your visit, it's essential to understand what to expect in terms of weather, so you can be prepared and make the most of your time in this beautiful city.

Summer (June - August):
Summer in Amsterdam is a delightful time to explore the city. The temperatures are relatively mild, with daytime highs averaging around 20-25°C (68-77°F). However, occasional heatwaves can push temperatures higher. It's a great time for outdoor activities, strolling along the canals, and enjoying the city's parks and terraces.

Autumn (September - November):

Autumn brings cooler temperatures and a touch of magic as the leaves change color. The weather can be quite variable, ranging from sunny days to drizzly ones. Daytime temperatures typically hover between 10-15°C (50-59°F), but be prepared for chilly evenings. It's an ideal season to experience Amsterdam's museums and cultural attractions.

Winter (December - February):

Winter in Amsterdam is chilly, with average daytime temperatures ranging from 2-6°C (36-43°F). While it rarely snows heavily, you might encounter some light snowfall. Don't forget to bundle up and explore the festive atmosphere with Christmas markets and cozy cafes. Some attractions may have shorter opening hours during this season, so plan your itinerary accordingly.

Spring (March - May):

Springtime is a wonderful season to visit Amsterdam, as the city awakens with blossoming flowers and greenery. Daytime temperatures gradually rise from 8-13°C (46-55°F) in March to 12-18°C (54-64°F) in May. The weather can be unpredictable, with occasional rain showers, but it's a refreshing time to experience the city's outdoor attractions, such as the Keukenhof Gardens showcasing vibrant tulip displays.

Rainfall:

Amsterdam experiences rainfall throughout the year, so it's always a good idea to carry a small umbrella or a waterproof jacket. The wettest months are usually August and October, so be prepared for occasional showers during your visit.

Tips for Dressing:

Layering is key: As the weather can be changeable, wear layers that you can add or remove as needed.

Comfortable shoes: Amsterdam is a walkable city, so comfortable shoes are essential for exploring.

Rain gear: Pack a small umbrella and a waterproof jacket to stay dry during rainy days.

Winter essentials: If visiting in winter, bring warm clothing, gloves, and a hat to keep cozy while outdoors.

Knowing about Amsterdam's weather will help you prepare well and enjoy your trip to the fullest. Whether it's hot or cold, Amsterdam's beauty and interesting places will create wonderful memories of this enchanting city that you'll never forget.

Necessary Entry Requirements and Visas

Before embarking on your journey to Amsterdam, it's crucial to familiarize yourself with the entry requirements and visa regulations that apply to your nationality. Ensuring you have the necessary travel documents in order will prevent any unexpected hurdles during your trip. Here's a simple guide to help you navigate the process:

European Union (EU) and Schengen Area Countries:

If you are a citizen of an EU or Schengen Area country, you can enter the Netherlands and stay in Amsterdam without a visa. The Schengen Area allows for free movement among its member states, which includes most EU countries and some non-EU countries like Norway, Switzerland, and Iceland. As long as you have a valid passport or national ID card, you can travel to Amsterdam for a short stay (usually up to 90 days within a 180-day period).

Visa-Free Countries:
Citizens of many countries, including the United States, Canada, Australia, and most European countries, do not require a visa for short stays in the Schengen Area, including the Netherlands. However, it's essential to check the specific visa waiver agreements that apply to your nationality to ensure eligibility.

Visa-Required Countries:
If you are from a country that is not in the EU, Schengen Area, or the visa-free list, you will need to apply for a Schengen visa to enter Amsterdam. The Schengen visa allows you to visit multiple Schengen countries, including the Netherlands, for a short stay. The visa application process may vary depending on your country of residence, so it's advisable to apply well in advance of your planned trip.

Visa-on-Arrival:
Some nationalities are eligible for a visa-on-arrival, which allows you to obtain a short-stay visa upon

arrival at Amsterdam's airport or border entry points. The visa-on-arrival typically grants a stay of up to 90 days within a 180-day period.

Visa Application:

If your nationality requires a visa to enter the Netherlands, you must apply for a Schengen visa at the Dutch embassy or consulate in your home country or the country where you legally reside. The application process may involve providing specific documents, such as proof of travel insurance, flight itinerary, accommodation reservations, and sufficient financial means to cover your stay.

Long-Term Stay and Residence Permits:

If you plan to stay in Amsterdam for an extended period, such as for work, study, or family reunification, different entry requirements and residence permits may apply. Depending on your purpose of stay, you will need to obtain the appropriate visa or residence permit before arriving in the Netherlands.

Passport Validity:

Ensure your passport is valid for at least six months beyond your intended departure date from the Schengen Area. Many countries have this requirement to avoid potential issues during your stay.

Always double-check the most up-to-date entry requirements and visa regulations before your departure, as they can change based on international agreements and policies. The official website of the Dutch government or the Netherlands' embassy in your country is a reliable source for the latest information.

Currency and Payment Options

When visiting Amsterdam, it's essential to become acquainted with the local currency and the most convenient payment options to ensure a smooth and hassle-free experience during your stay. Here's a simple guide to help you handle your finances in the city:

Local Currency:

The official currency of the Netherlands is the Euro (€). Banknotes come in denominations of €5, €10, €20, €50, €100, €200, and €500, while coins are available in 1, 2, 5, 10, 20, and 50 cents, as well as €1 and €2.

Cash Usage:

Although credit and debit cards are widely accepted, it's a good idea to carry some cash, especially for smaller purchases and in case you visit places that may not accept cards. ATMs (Automated Teller Machines) are readily available throughout Amsterdam, allowing you to withdraw Euros using your debit or credit card. Just be aware that some ATMs may charge additional fees for international withdrawals.

Credit and Debit Cards:

Credit and debit cards, especially Visa and Mastercard, are widely accepted in Amsterdam. Many restaurants, shops, and tourist attractions offer card payment options. However, it's always a good idea to inform your bank about your travel plans to ensure smooth card transactions and avoid any potential blocks due to suspected fraud.

Contactless Payments:
Contactless payments are widely used in Amsterdam, and you'll find that many establishments accept them for purchases up to a certain amount. Just tap your contactless-enabled card or smartphone on the payment terminal to complete your transaction quickly.

Currency Exchange:
If you need to exchange foreign currency for Euros, you can do so at currency exchange offices (often called "GWK Travelex") at major airports, train stations, or in the city center. Be mindful of the exchange rates and any additional fees that might apply.

Tipping Culture:
Tipping is not mandatory in Amsterdam, as service charges are usually included in bills at restaurants and cafes. However, leaving a small tip for exceptional service is appreciated. A tip of 5-10% is

customary if you feel inclined to show your appreciation.

Currency Conversion Apps:
Consider using currency conversion apps on your smartphone to quickly check the current exchange rates and track your expenses in your home currency.

To confidently manage your finances during your stay in Amsterdam, familiarizing yourself with the local currency and best payment methods, you can.

Language and Basic Phrases

While English is widely spoken and understood in Amsterdam, learning a few basic Dutch phrases can go a long way in enhancing your travel experience and showing appreciation for the local culture.

The Dutch are known for their warmth and friendliness, and making an effort to speak their language, even just a little, will surely be appreciated. Here are some simple and useful Dutch phrases to get you started:

Hello - Hallo (hah-loh)

Good morning - Goedemorgen (khoo-duh-mawr-khun)

Good afternoon - Goedemiddag (khoo-duh-mih-dahkh)

Good evening - Goedenavond (khoo-duh-nah-vohnt)

Thank you - Dank je wel (dahnk yuh vell) / Dank u wel (dahnk oo vell - more formal)

Please - Alstublieft (ahl-stu-bleeft)

Excuse me - Excuseer mij (ehk-skew-seer may)

Yes - Ja (yah)

No - Nee (nay)

How much does this cost? - Hoeveel kost dit? (hoo-vale kost dit?)

Where is the bathroom? - Waar is de badkamer? (vahr is duh bahd-kah-mur)

I don't understand - Ik begrijp het niet (ik buh-khreyp hut neet)

Can you speak English? - Spreekt u Engels? (spraykt uu enguls?)

Help! - Help! (hehlp)

Remember to speak slowly and clearly, and don't worry if your pronunciation isn't perfect. The locals will appreciate your effort to communicate in Dutch, no matter how simple your phrases may be.

Pro Tip: Many Dutch people are multilingual, and you'll find that they often switch to English if they notice you're struggling with Dutch. However, don't be discouraged! Politely expressing your desire to practice Dutch may encourage them to speak more in the local language.

Learning a few basic Dutch phrases will not only help you in everyday interactions, such as ordering food at a restaurant or asking for directions, but it will also add a personal touch to your travel experience.

Amsterdam City's Public Transportation System and How to Get Around

Amsterdam offers an efficient and well-connected public transportation system that makes exploring the city a breeze. Understanding the various transportation options and how to get around will help you make the most of your time in Amsterdam. Here's a simple guide to navigating the city's public transportation:

Trams: Trams are a popular mode of transportation in Amsterdam and cover most parts of the city. They run frequently, making it easy to hop on and off to reach various attractions and neighborhoods. Look for tram stops marked with the blue and white "GVB" logo, and remember to check the tram numbers and directions before boarding.

Buses: Amsterdam's bus network complements the tram system and reaches areas that trams may not cover. Buses are an excellent option for traveling to destinations outside the city center. Look for bus stops with the "GVB" logo or specific bus numbers.

Metro: The Amsterdam metro system is not as extensive as the tram and bus networks but is efficient for traveling to the city's outskirts or major train stations. Metro stations are marked with the "M" logo.

GVB Tickets: To use the trams, buses, and metro, you can purchase GVB tickets from ticket machines at major stations, GVB ticket counters, or online.

Single-use tickets are available for a specific duration (e.g., 1 hour, 1 day) or as multi-day passes. If you plan to use public transportation frequently, consider buying a multi-day pass, as it offers better value for money.

OV-Chipkaart: An alternative to single-use tickets is the OV-chipkaart, a rechargeable public transport card. You can load credit onto the card and use it for seamless travel on all GVB services as well as other Dutch public transport providers.

Biking: Biking is an incredibly popular way to get around Amsterdam, as the city is bike-friendly with dedicated bike lanes. You can rent bikes from various rental shops and explore the city at your own pace.

Taxis: Taxis are readily available, but they can be relatively expensive compared to public transportation. They are a convenient option if you prefer door-to-door service or for late-night travel when public transport services are less frequent.

Ferries: Amsterdam is intersected by several free ferries that transport pedestrians and cyclists across the IJ River to different parts of the city. These ferries offer fantastic views of the city skyline and are a unique part of Amsterdam's transportation system.

Chapter Two

Where to Stay

A s you plan your stay in Amsterdam, you'll find a wide array of accommodation options catering to all budgets and preferences. Whether you're a budget-conscious traveler or seeking a luxurious experience, Amsterdam has something to offer for everyone. Here's a simple guide to help you discover the best places to stay:

Budget Hostels:

For budget travelers and backpackers, Amsterdam boasts a vibrant hostel scene. These hostels offer affordable dormitory-style accommodations, communal spaces to meet fellow travelers, and often provide various amenities such as free Wi-Fi, communal kitchens, and organized social events. Staying in a hostel is an excellent way to make new friends and share travel experiences.

Cozy Bed and Breakfasts:

Amsterdam is known for its charming bed and breakfasts (B&Bs). These cozy accommodations are typically run by friendly hosts who provide personalized service and local insights. B&Bs often offer comfortable rooms with unique touches and delicious homemade breakfasts to start your day off right.

Mid-Range Hotels:

If you're looking for a comfortable stay without breaking the bank, mid-range hotels in Amsterdam are a popular choice. These hotels provide a range of amenities such as private bathrooms, room service, and on-site restaurants. You'll have a comfortable base to explore the city while enjoying good value for your money.

Boutique Hotels:

Amsterdam is dotted with stylish boutique hotels that offer a blend of modern design and personalized service. These intimate properties often have a unique theme or concept, making your stay a memorable experience. Boutique hotels are ideal for those seeking a touch of luxury with a distinctive ambiance.

Luxury Hotels:

For travelers who crave the finest accommodations and exceptional service, Amsterdam boasts a selection of luxury hotels that cater to every desire. These 5-star properties offer lavish rooms, gourmet dining options, spa facilities, and top-notch amenities to ensure an unforgettable stay.

Apartment Rentals:

If you prefer the convenience of a home-away-from-home, consider renting an apartment in Amsterdam. Apartment rentals provide more space, a kitchen, and the flexibility to create your own schedule. It's an excellent option for families, groups, or travelers seeking an extended stay.

Unique Stays:

In Amsterdam, you can also find unique accommodation options, such as houseboats floating on the picturesque canals or traditional canal houses converted into charming guesthouses. These one-of-a-kind stays offer a glimpse into Amsterdam's distinctive culture and architecture.

When booking your accommodation, consider factors such as location, proximity to public transportation, and the amenities that best suit your needs. With a diverse range of options, Amsterdam ensures that you'll find the perfect place to stay, tailored to your preferences and budget, for an unforgettable experience in this captivating city.

Chapter Three

Top Attractions and Activities

The Van Gogh Museum

Nestled in the heart of Amsterdam, the Van Gogh Museum stands as a captivating tribute to the life and artistry of one of the world's most renowned artists, Vincent van Gogh. This iconic museum offers visitors an immersive experience, delving deep into the brilliant mind and profound emotions that shaped Van Gogh's extraordinary masterpieces.

The Van Gogh Museum houses the largest collection of artworks by Vincent van Gogh, featuring over 200 paintings, 500 drawings, and 700 letters penned by the artist himself. Step into a world of vibrant colors and powerful brushstrokes as you encounter iconic works like "Sunflowers," "The Bedroom," and "Almond Blossom." Witness Van Gogh's artistic journey, from his early works to his mesmerizing post-impressionist creations.

Beyond the artworks, the museum offers a unique opportunity to explore the life and struggles of Vincent van Gogh. Gain insights into his personal correspondence, which provides a poignant glimpse into his thoughts and emotions. Learn about the challenges he faced, his relentless pursuit of artistic expression, and the profound impact he left on the art world.

The Van Gogh Museum hosts engaging exhibitions that shed light on various aspects of Van Gogh's life and artistic development. These temporary exhibits often showcase the artist's works alongside those of his contemporaries, enriching the context and appreciation of his artistic legacy.

The museum provides a dynamic and interactive experience for visitors of all ages. Audio guides, multimedia displays, and guided tours offer informative and engaging insights into Van Gogh's art and life, making the museum accessible and enjoyable for art enthusiasts and casual visitors alike.

Take a piece of Van Gogh's art with you by exploring the well-curated museum shop, where you can find art prints, books, and unique souvenirs inspired by the artist's work. After immersing yourself in the world of Van Gogh, relax and reflect in one of the museum's cozy cafes, offering a delightful selection of refreshments.

A visit to the Van Gogh Museum is a profound and moving experience, allowing you to connect with the artist on a personal level and gain a deeper appreciation for his remarkable contributions to the world of art.

Rijksmuseum

Situated in Amsterdam's Museum Square, the Rijksmuseum stands as a majestic beacon of Dutch history and art. This world-class museum offers a captivating journey through the centuries, inviting visitors to explore the richness of Dutch culture and heritage.

As you step into the Rijksmuseum, you embark on a voyage through time. The museum's vast collection features over 8,000 objects, showcasing Dutch history from the Middle Ages to the present day. Discover historical artifacts, including rare documents, fascinating weaponry, and intricately crafted furniture, which offer unique insights into the country's past.

The Rijksmuseum is renowned for its exceptional collection of Golden Age art, a period of unprecedented prosperity and cultural flourishing in the Netherlands during the 17th century. Feast your eyes on iconic masterpieces by Dutch masters such as Rembrandt, Vermeer, and Frans Hals. Be captivated by Rembrandt's "The Night Watch" and Vermeer's "The Milkmaid," as they showcase the artists' brilliance and mastery of light and shadow.

Immerse yourself in the beauty of Delftware, the famous blue-and-white ceramics that became synonymous with Dutch craftsmanship. Admire delicate porcelain, dazzling glassware, and exquisite textiles that adorn the museum's galleries, reflecting the Netherlands' rich tradition of decorative arts.

In addition to its Dutch treasures, the Rijksmuseum houses an exceptional collection of Asian art, including captivating objects from Indonesia, China, Japan, and beyond. These artifacts illustrate the global connections forged by Dutch trade and cultural exchanges during the Golden Age.

Beyond its artistic riches, the Rijksmuseum boasts stunning gardens and remarkable architecture. The museum's Gothic and Renaissance Revival-style building is an architectural masterpiece in itself, designed by Pierre Cuypers. Take a leisurely stroll through the beautifully landscaped gardens, adding a serene touch to your museum experience.

The Rijksmuseum caters to visitors of all ages, offering engaging family programs and activities. Children can embark on captivating treasure hunts, art workshops, and interactive exhibits, making the museum a delightful destination for families.

A visit to the Rijksmuseum is an immersive encounter with the soul of Dutch history, art, and culture. As you wander through its grand halls, you'll be transported through time and witness the incredible achievements of the Dutch people.

Anne Frank House

A visit to the Anne Frank House in Amsterdam is a poignant and moving experience, offering a glimpse into the life of Anne Frank and her family during one of the darkest periods in history, World War II.

The Anne Frank House is situated in the heart of Amsterdam, at Prinsengracht 263, where the Frank family sought refuge during the Nazi occupation of the Netherlands. The house has been preserved as a museum, allowing visitors to step back in time and bear witness to the courage and resilience of Anne and her family.

As you explore the Anne Frank House, you'll have the opportunity to enter the secret annex where Anne, her parents, sister, and four other Jewish people hid from the persecution of the Nazis. The cramped quarters, concealed behind a bookshelf, stand as a testament to the challenges and fears faced by those seeking safety during the Holocaust.

Anne Frank's diary, "The Diary of a Young Girl," is an integral part of the museum experience. The diary, filled with Anne's thoughts, dreams, and emotions, has become a symbol of hope and resilience in the face of adversity. As you read her words and reflect on her poignant insights, you'll gain a deeper understanding of the impact of the Holocaust on a young girl's life.

Although the Anne Frank House is a solemn reminder of the atrocities of war, it also carries a powerful message of hope, resilience, and the importance of embracing diversity and human rights. Anne's legacy continues to inspire generations, reminding us of the importance of compassion and the pursuit of a more just and tolerant world.

The museum offers educational exhibits and displays that shed light on the historical context of World War II and the persecution of Jewish people during the Holocaust. These exhibits provide essential context to Anne Frank's story and help visitors understand the broader impact of the war on Amsterdam and its residents.

Due to its popularity, the Anne Frank House operates on a timed entry ticket system. It's essential to book your tickets in advance to secure your visit and ensure a meaningful and contemplative experience without overcrowding.

A visit to the Anne Frank House is a journey of remembrance, reflection, and gratitude for the lessons of history. It is a solemn reminder of the resilience of the human spirit and an invitation to embrace the values of tolerance, empathy, and compassion. As you walk through the rooms where Anne Frank penned her thoughts and dreams, you'll be touched by the enduring impact of her story and the need to protect and cherish the principles of freedom and equality for all.

A Canal Cruise

Embark on a delightful adventure in Amsterdam by taking a canal cruise along the city's iconic waterways. A canal cruise offers a unique and relaxing way to experience the charm and beauty of Amsterdam from a different perspective.

Amsterdam's canals are not just picturesque; they are an integral part of the city's history and culture. Known as the "Venice of the North," Amsterdam boasts a network of intricate canals, flanked by elegant bridges and stunning architecture. During your canal cruise, you'll have the opportunity to marvel at the city's UNESCO-listed canal ring, a proof of Amsterdam's rich heritage.

As the boat glides gently along the water, you'll be treated to enchanting views of Amsterdam's historic buildings, gabled houses, and quaint houseboats lining the canals. The city's beauty truly comes to life from the water, allowing you to capture postcard-worthy moments and create lasting memories.

A canal cruise offers a tranquil and leisurely experience, perfect for unwinding after a day of exploration. Sit back, relax, and enjoy the soothing rhythm of the water as you pass by some of Amsterdam's most iconic landmarks.

There are various canal cruise options to choose from, catering to different preferences. Whether you prefer a classic open boat, a glass-topped boat offering unobstructed views, or a cozy evening cruise with dinner and drinks, you'll find a cruise that suits your style.

Most canal cruises come with informative commentary available in multiple languages. Listen to fascinating stories and historical facts about Amsterdam, adding depth and context to the sights you see along the way.

For a truly enchanting experience, consider taking an evening canal cruise during sunset. Amsterdam's canals come alive with warm hues, creating a magical ambiance that will leave you in awe.

Each canal cruise offers its own unique route, allowing you to discover different parts of the city and experience Amsterdam from various perspectives. Some cruises may take you to hidden gems and less-visited corners, offering a glimpse into the city's local life.

Vondelpark

In the middle of Amsterdam, you'll find Vondelpark, a peaceful place where you can escape the city's busy life and enjoy nature's beauty. This park is loved by both locals and visitors, offering lots of things to do for a fun day outdoors.

Vondelpark is a big, green space with well-kept lawns, pretty ponds, and beautiful flowers. It's a calm and relaxing place, perfect for unwinding and taking it easy.

Bring your favorite snacks and have a lovely picnic with your friends or family on the grass. You can bring your own food or get something tasty from the nearby cafés. Picnics in Vondelpark are a favorite activity for many people.

You can rent a bike and explore the park's paths and tree-lined streets. Riding a bike in Vondelpark is a great way to see all the nice parts of the park and feel the fresh air. You can easily find bikes for rent near the park entrances and enjoy a leisurely bike ride at your own pace.

Take a slow walk in Vondelpark and enjoy being close to nature. The park's beauty and peaceful atmosphere will make your walk very refreshing.

You'll see joggers, families, and couples having a good time in this lovely park.

Sometimes, Vondelpark hosts special events like outdoor concerts, theater shows, and cultural festivals. If you check the park's schedule, you might find some exciting events happening during your visit, making your time in the park even more enjoyable.

Families with kids will have a lot of fun at Vondelpark's playgrounds. Kids can run, climb, and play in these safe and enjoyable play areas.

One special thing about the park is the Vondelpark Openluchttheater, an open-air theater where musicians, dancers, and performers show off their talents. You can enjoy spontaneous music or cultural shows under the open sky, creating lasting memories of your visit.

Jordaan District

The streets of Jordaan is a must visit spot for both tourists and locals, it offers a delightful mix of history, art and vibrant culture. Every corner of this street holds hidden treasures and surprises, making each stroll an adventure of its own.

Jordaan is an artistic hub, filled with numerous art galleries and studios that showcase the creativity of local artists. Take your time exploring their masterpieces and unique creations, and be inspired by the district's lively art scene.

When you need a break, head to one of Jordaan's cozy cafes and eateries for some relaxation. Treat yourself to freshly brewed coffee, delectable pastries, or traditional Dutch delights. The welcoming atmosphere of these cafes is the perfect escape from your explorations.

For a tranquil moment, head to the canal-side and enjoy a leisurely stroll or simply sit on a bench and watch boats glide along the water. It's a peaceful oasis amidst the bustling city center.

Jordaan also offers lively markets and charming boutiques where you can find unique treasures and local souvenirs. Whether you're into vintage shops or trendy boutiques, you're sure to discover something special to take home.

As you explore Jordaan, you'll come across historical landmarks that share the neighborhood's rich past. The impressive Westerkerk, with its towering spire, is one of Jordaan's prominent landmarks that showcase its historical significance.

Throughout the year, Jordaan hosts various festivals and events that celebrate local culture and traditions. Check the schedule during your visit, and you might get a chance to experience the vibrant community spirit through these authentic and festive gatherings.

Red Light District

The Red-Light District is an area with a lot of history and plays a significant role in the city's society.

First of all, remember to approach the Red-Light District with respect and an open mind. It's not just about the red-lit windows; there's much more to learn and understand. Take some time to explore its cultural background and how it has evolved over time.

Beyond the initial impression, the Red-Light District is a diverse neighborhood with all kinds of businesses, like cafes, restaurants, shops, and theaters. It gives you a taste of Amsterdam's vibrant and cosmopolitan character.

When you visit, make sure to be respectful of the people who live and work there, especially the sex workers. Avoid taking photos or intruding on their privacy. They're individuals with their own stories and experiences.

If you want to learn even more about the district's culture, consider taking a guided tour with a local guide. They can provide valuable insights and help you navigate the area respectfully.

Like in any busy area, be mindful of your safety and keep an eye on your belongings. It's always good to travel with others and avoid getting involved in any illegal or risky activities.

The Red-Light District might challenge some cultural norms, but keeping an open mind will help you appreciate the diversity and complexities of Amsterdam's society. Embrace understanding different perspectives and experiences.

Remember, Amsterdam has so much more to offer beyond the Red-Light District. Take the chance to explore other neighborhoods, museums, parks, and cultural sites that make this city so special.

Where to Eat

Dutch Traditional Dishes

When in the Netherlands, treating your taste buds to the delightful flavors of Dutch cuisine is a must! From sweet treats to savory snacks, the Dutch have a range of traditional dishes that will leave you craving for more.

Stroopwafels:

One of the all-time favorites is stroopwafels - thin waffle cookies filled with delicious caramel. You'll find them freshly made and warm at local markets and bakeries. Take a bite, and you'll be hooked by the sweet, gooey caramel in the middle.

Herring:

For a true taste of the sea, give Dutch herring a try. This traditional fish dish is often served with chopped onions and pickles. Don't worry if you're not a fan of fish – herring in the Netherlands is usually mild and surprisingly delicious, even for those new to it.

Bitterballen:

Craving something savory? Look no further than bitterballen. These bite-sized croquettes are filled with a creamy mixture of beef and spices. A popular treat at Dutch pubs, locals love to enjoy them with a side of mustard.

Poffertjes:

Imagine fluffy mini pancakes dusted with powdered sugar – that's poffertjes! These delightful sweet treats are a staple at Dutch street markets and festivals. Served warm with a dollop of butter, poffertjes are a delight for kids and adults alike.

Stamppot:

For a heartier meal, savor the traditional Dutch dish called stamppot. It consists of mashed potatoes mixed with various vegetables. One of the most famous varieties is "Boerenkool" stamppot, which includes mashed potatoes and kale, served with smoked sausage on top.

Dutch Cheese:
Cheese enthusiasts, rejoice! The Netherlands is famous for its delectable cheeses like Gouda and Edam. Head to a local cheese shop to sample some unique flavors and take home a taste of Dutch cheese culture.

Dutch Pancakes:
Last but `not least, don't miss out on the Dutch pancakes, or "pannenkoeken." These large, thin pancakes offer a world of possibilities. Enjoy them with sweet toppings like powdered sugar, fruit, or syrup, or try savory options like cheese and bacon.

Best Restaurants and Food Markets

When it comes to food, Amsterdam has an incredible array of dining options that will tantalize your taste buds and satisfy any craving. From local delicacies to international delights, the city's restaurants and food markets offer a gastronomic adventure like no other.

International Cuisine:

Embark on a culinary journey around the world without leaving Amsterdam. The city boasts a diverse dining scene with restaurants offering cuisines from all corners of the globe. Whether you're craving sushi from Japan, mouthwatering curries from India, flavorful pasta from Italy, or exotic flavors from the Middle East, you're sure to find it all in Amsterdam.

Dutch Delicacies:

Don't miss the chance to sample some authentic Dutch delicacies. Taste traditional dishes like erwtensoep (pea soup), kroketten (croquettes), and pannenkoeken (pancakes). For a sweet treat, indulge in stroopwafels, speculaas cookies, or a Dutch apple pie.

Food Markets:

For a true foodie experience, explore Amsterdam's bustling food markets. Albert Cuyp Market, the city's most famous street market, offers a fantastic array of fresh produce, street food, and snacks. The Foodhallen, a converted tram depot, is a foodie paradise with a wide selection of food stalls serving everything from gourmet burgers to Asian street food.

Michelin-Starred Excellence:

For a fine dining experience, Amsterdam boasts several Michelin-starred restaurants. Treat yourself to an exquisite meal prepared by world-class chefs, and savor innovative dishes that blend traditional flavors with modern techniques.

Waterfront Dining:

Enjoy a unique dining experience with waterfront restaurants along Amsterdam's canals. The scenic views and relaxed ambiance make for a memorable meal, whether you're indulging in a leisurely lunch or a romantic dinner.

Hidden Gems:

Amsterdam is full of hidden gems, from cozy neighborhood eateries to tucked-away cafes. These local favorites often offer a more intimate and authentic dining experience, allowing you to savor the city's culinary delights like a true local.

Food Festivals and Events:

Keep an eye out for food festivals and events happening throughout the year. These gatherings celebrate Amsterdam's vibrant food culture, offering a chance to taste a wide range of dishes and culinary creations.

Vegan and Vegetarian Delights

Calling all vegans and vegetarians! Amsterdam is a paradise for plant-based eaters, offering a vibrant and diverse food scene that celebrates cruelty-free and delicious dining options.

Vegan Cuisine Galore:

In Amsterdam, you'll find a wide array of vegan restaurants and eateries that cater to every palate. From delectable vegan burgers and scrumptious plant-based pizzas to flavorful Asian-inspired dishes and hearty vegan comfort food, the city's culinary landscape has it all.

Veggie-Friendly Cafes:

Even non-vegans will appreciate the veggie-friendly cafes that serve up creative and healthy vegetarian options. These cafes offer an abundance of fresh salads, tasty sandwiches, and nourishing bowls, providing a delightful and guilt-free feast.

Vegan Sweet Treats:
Indulge your sweet tooth with an assortment of vegan pastries, cakes, and desserts that are sure to satisfy any craving. From luscious vegan cheesecakes to fluffy vegan pancakes, these sweet treats are a must-try for everyone, regardless of dietary preferences.

Sustainable and Ethical:
Amsterdam's plant-based food scene often embraces sustainability and ethical practices. Many vegan and vegetarian establishments source their ingredients locally and strive to reduce their ecological footprint, making dining in the city a deliciously conscious choice.

Vegan-Friendly Markets:
Explore Amsterdam's markets, where you'll discover an abundance of fresh produce, vegan snacks, and plant-based goodies. Some markets even have dedicated stalls selling vegan street food, making them a food lover's paradise.

Vegan Street Food:
Don't miss the chance to try some mouthwatering vegan street food, which is becoming increasingly

popular in Amsterdam. From falafel wraps and vegan tacos to savory vegan stroopwafels, these food trucks and stalls offer on-the-go delights for hungry travelers.

Vegan Fusion Cuisine:
Amsterdam's food scene often blends various culinary traditions, creating exciting vegan fusion dishes that push the boundaries of flavor. Discover delightful combinations that marry global tastes with innovative plant-based ingredients.

Nightlife and Entertainment

Bars and Pubs:

When the sun goes down, Amsterdam's nightlife comes alive! Step into the city's best bars and pubs to experience the buzz and excitement. From trendy cocktail lounges to cozy brown cafes, there's something for everyone. Sip on classic Dutch beers or try inventive cocktails crafted by talented mixologists. Enjoy the lively atmosphere and make new friends as you soak in the vibrant nightlife of Amsterdam.

Concerts and Music Venues:

Music lovers, rejoice! Amsterdam boasts a thriving music scene with a plethora of concert venues that host performances to suit all tastes. Catch live gigs by local bands, international artists, and renowned musicians. Whether you're into rock, jazz, electronic, or classical music, the city has a venue that will get you grooving to the beat.

Coffeeshops:

Amsterdam is famous for its unique approach to cannabis consumption, and coffeeshops play a part in this culture. Before you visit, it's essential to understand the legal regulations surrounding cannabis. Coffeeshops offer a range of cannabis products, from pre-rolled joints to edibles. If you're curious to try, approach it responsibly and be aware of the guidelines for a safe and enjoyable experience.

Day Trips from Amsterdam

J oin the most delightful adventure as we explore some fantastic day trips from the enchanting city of Amsterdam! No matter if you're passionate about history, a nature enthusiast, or just in need of a change of scenery, these nearby destinations offer something special for everyone.

Zaanse Schans: A Step Back in Time

Just a short distance from Amsterdam, Zaanse Schans is a charming open-air museum that takes you back in time to the Dutch Golden Age. Here, you'll find picturesque windmills set against a serene countryside backdrop. Watch the wooden clogs being crafted, taste delicious Dutch cheeses, and witness the traditional way of making mustard.

Zaanse Schans offers a perfect blend of history and culture.

Keukenhof Gardens: A Floral Paradise

For flower enthusiasts, a visit to Keukenhof Gardens is a must. Located just outside Amsterdam, this botanical wonderland boasts a spectacular display of colorful tulips, daffodils, hyacinths, and other blooms. Stroll through the well-designed gardens, take in the fragrant air, and capture Instagram-worthy shots amidst the vibrant sea of flowers.

Utrecht: Canals and Charm

Hop on a short train ride to Utrecht, a city that will capture your heart with its charming canals and rich history. Take a boat tour along the picturesque waterways and marvel at the unique wharf cellars that have been converted into shops and restaurants. Don't forget to climb the Dom Tower for panoramic views of the city, rewarding you for the climb with an unforgettable experience.

Haarlem: Art and Culture

Just a stone's throw away from Amsterdam lies Haarlem, a city with a thriving arts and cultural scene. Explore the impressive Frans Hals Museum, home to Dutch Golden Age masterpieces, and wander through the quaint cobblestone streets dotted with boutique shops and inviting cafes. Haarlem's relaxed atmosphere makes it a perfect spot to unwind and savor the local life.

Rotterdam: Modern Marvels

For a taste of contemporary Dutch architecture and urban vibes, venture to Rotterdam, the architectural playground of the Netherlands. This city boasts an array of eye-catching modern buildings and stunning skyscrapers. Take a walk along the striking Erasmus Bridge, visit the futuristic Cube Houses, and explore the vibrant Markthal, a food market housed in an extraordinary arched building.

The Hague: Royal and Political Hub

Discover the political heart of the Netherlands in The Hague, home to the Dutch government and the royal family. Admire the impressive Binnenhof, where the Dutch Parliament convenes, and explore the Mauritshuis Museum, which houses Vermeer's iconic "Girl with a Pearl Earring." Take a leisurely stroll on the sandy beaches of Scheveningen and enjoy the seaside charm.

Giethoorn: Venice of the North

Prepare to be amazed by the fairytale-like village of Giethoorn, often referred to as the "Venice of the North." With no roads, this idyllic place is only accessible by boat or foot, and its picturesque canals and thatched-roof cottages will transport you to a magical world. Rent a traditional "whisper boat" and navigate the peaceful waterways at your own pace.

Each of these day trips from Amsterdam promises an unforgettable experience, adding new dimensions to your Dutch adventure.

Tips for an Unforgettable Trip

Traveling sustainably is not only about having a great adventure but also about caring for the environment and the places you visit. Here are some simple tips to make your journey greener and more responsible:

Say No to Single-Use Plastics:
Bring a reusable water bottle and fill it up at water fountains or stations. This way, you can avoid using plastic bottles that create unnecessary waste. Also, bring a reusable shopping bag to skip using plastic bags during your trip.

Choose Eco-Friendly Accommodation:
Look for hotels or places to stay that care about the environment. Check for eco-certifications or initiatives that show they support sustainable practices.

Support Local Businesses:

When eating, shopping, or planning activities, go for local businesses that promote sustainability. Pick restaurants that serve locally sourced and organic food. Buying souvenirs from local artisans not only supports their livelihoods but also helps preserve the local culture.

Save Energy and Water:

Be mindful of your energy usage in your accommodation. Remember to turn off lights and electronics when not needed, and use air conditioning and heating responsibly. If you're in a place with limited water supply, try to conserve water by taking shorter showers and reusing towels.

Use Public Transportation or Walk:

Whenever you can, use public transportation, walk, or bike around. These eco-friendly options reduce carbon emissions and let you experience the destination more intimately. Biking, for instance, is a popular and sustainable way to explore places like Amsterdam.

Respect Wildlife and Nature:

Keep a safe distance from wildlife and avoid feeding or touching them. If you want to participate in wildlife tours, choose ones that prioritize animal welfare and conservation. Stick to marked trails and respect protected areas to preserve the natural beauty of the environment.

Dispose of Waste Properly:

Always use designated bins or recycling facilities for your trash. Never litter and be respectful of the local environment. If you come across litter during your travels, consider joining a local clean-up event to help keep the area clean.

Learn About Local Culture and Customs:

Take the time to learn about the culture and traditions of the places you visit. Respect the local customs, dress codes, and etiquette as a way of showing appreciation for their way of life.

By following these sustainable travel tips and being a responsible traveler, you can make a positive impact on the destinations you explore, ensuring they remain beautiful and enjoyable for future generations.

Appendix

Essential Contact Information

Emergency Services (Police, Fire, Ambulance): 112

Tourist Police: +31 20 244 9999

U.S. Embassy in Amsterdam: +31 70 310 2209

Canadian Embassy in The Hague: +31 70 311 1600

British Consulate General in Amsterdam: +31 20 676 4343

Australian Embassy in The Hague: +31 70 310 8200

Public Holidays in the Netherlands (2023)

New Year's Day - January 1

Easter Sunday - April 9

Easter Monday - April 10

King's Day - April 27

Liberation Day - May 5

Ascension Day - May 18

Pentecost - May 28

Whit Monday - June 5

Christmas Day - December 25

Boxing Day - December 26

Printed in Great Britain
by Amazon